DISCOVERING
Everyday Things

Lion Publishing

In God's world,
even the little everyday things
are beautiful.

Hold up your finger and look at it closely.
It is marked with a pattern of lines.
There are millions of people on the earth,
but not one of them has
the same pattern on his finger-tips.
It is your own special design.

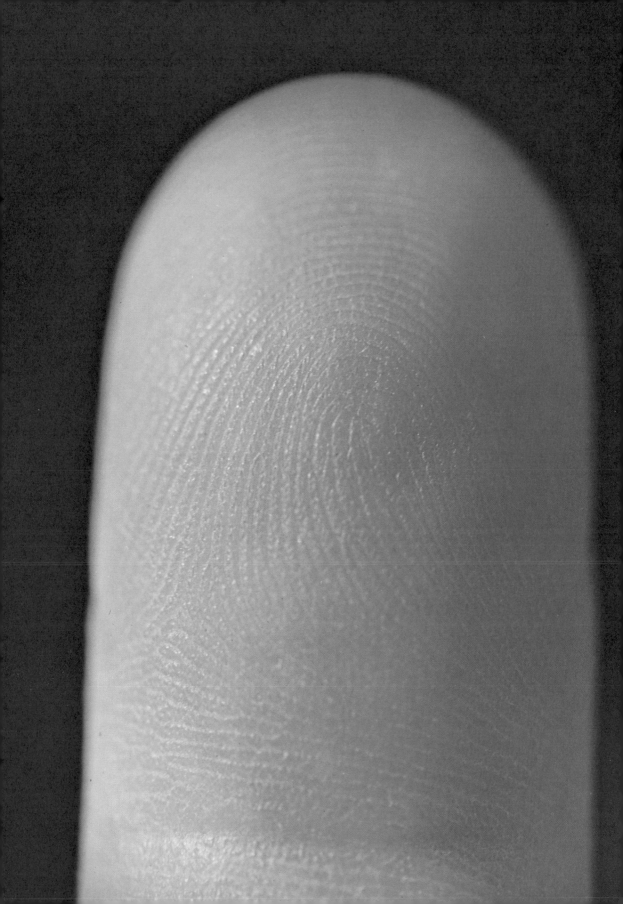

Here's a funny thing, it's all lumps and bumps. What do you think it is?

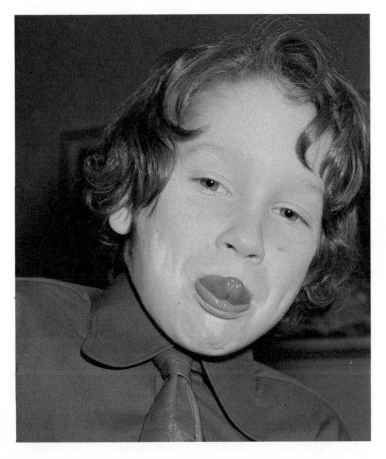

It's the end of your tongue!
Put your tongue out at a mirror
and you will see the bumps.
They are very sensitive, and help you
taste things.

This butterfly's wing is made up
of little scales, like feathers.
They all fit together like this.

Each one is in the right place
to make up the beautiful colours that we see.
If you touch a butterfly's wing
the scales come off on your fingers like
fine dust, and the wing is spoilt.

Have you seen the long whiskers
on a rabbit's nose?
They are very important
because he can feel things with them,
rather like we do with our fingers.

10

This is not yellow grass,
but a field full of little yellow flowers.
Can you count them?
Each flower looks like this.

Think how many there must be
in just one field!

A feather is held together with hooks,
thousands of them on each frond.
See if you can find a cast-off feather
and look at it closely.

If you pull the fronds apart,
you will feel the hooks gripping.

This is a dragonfly.
You can see him flying around in summer.
If you could get close enough
you would see that he has great big eyes.

Each eye is made up of patterns like this.

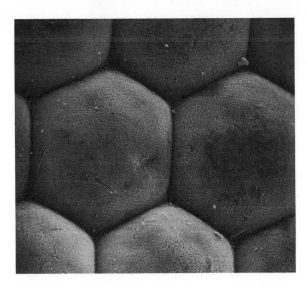

17

Stones look very ordinary,
lying in the garden. But if you ask
someone to break them in half for you
and then wet them or paint them with
clear varnish, you will see some of the
colours that are hiding inside.

18

Have you ever seen little round eggs like this one on a leaf?
They may have been laid by a butterfly or a moth. Each one has a different pattern, like this moth's egg.

Leaves come in every shape and size you can imagine. They also have a pattern on them made by the veins. In spring and summer they are green. In autumn they turn brown and gold. See how many different shapes and colours you can find.

This is a bee visiting a flower.
Can you see the pollen from the flower
all over his back legs like dust?
Close up, each speck of pollen dust
has a lovely pattern like this.

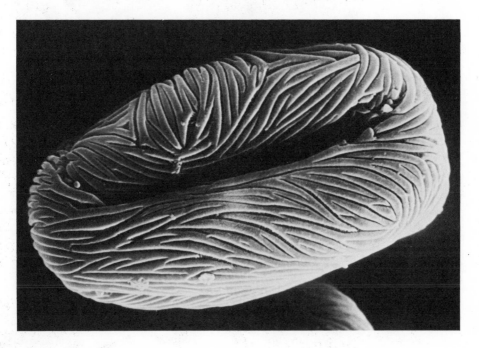

The pollen from each flower
has a different pattern.

If you could look very closely
at just one drop of pond water,
you would see thousands of tiny plants
and animals.

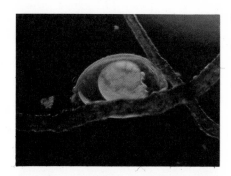

This is a snail's egg.
You can see right
through it.

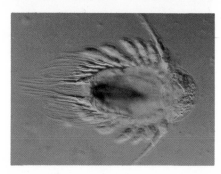

This is a tiny crab.

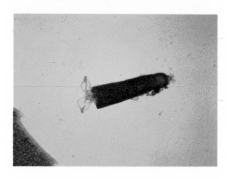

This animal lives
in a tube.
He moves about by
wiggling the paddles
you can see in the
picture.

God has made such a wonderful world
full of patterns and colours.
He has given us eyes to see and enjoy
them.
Look around carefully and you may
discover some more surprises for
yourself.